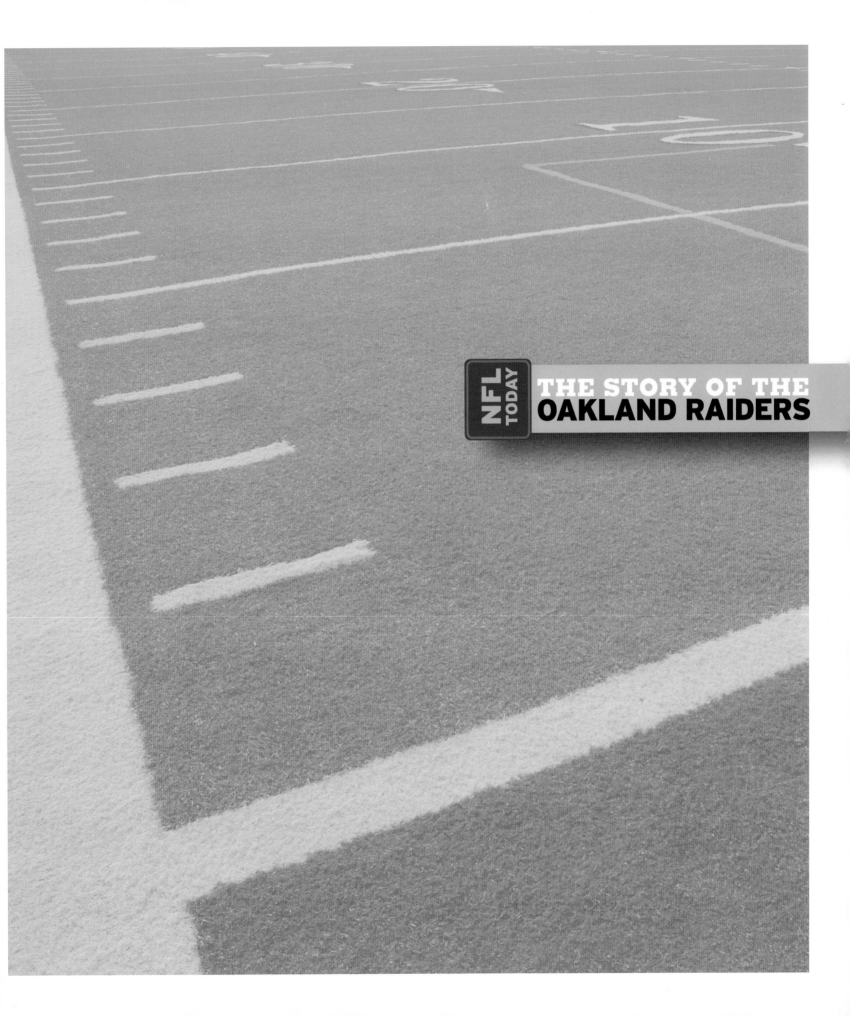

NFL
TODAY

THE STORY OF THE
OAKLAND RAIDERS

NFL TODAY

THE STORY OF THE OAKLAND RAIDERS

SCOTT CAFFREY

CREATIVE EDUCATION

Cover: Quarterback JaMarcus Russell (top), guard
Gene Upshaw (bottom)
Page 2: Center Jim Otto
Pages 4–5: Defensive end Derrick Burgess
Pages 6–7: Raiders offensive linemen, 1977

....

Published by Creative Education
P.O. Box 227, Mankato, Minnesota 56002
Creative Education is an imprint of
The Creative Company
www.thecreativecompany.us

Design and production by Blue Design
Design Associate: Sarah Yakawonis
Printed in the United States of America

Photographs by Corbis (Bettmann), Getty Images
(Brian Bahr, B. Bennett, Morris Berman/NFL,
Bernstein Associates, Stephen Dunn, John Elk III,
James Flores/NFL, Focus On Sport, George Long/
NFL, John G. Mabanglo/AFP, Takashi Makita/NFL,
Al Messerschmidt/NFL, Ronald C. Modra/Sports
Imagery, NFL, Mike Powell, Pro Football Hall of
Fame/NFL, Joe Robbins, Paul Spinelli, Jamie Squire,
Kevin Terrell, Greg Trott, Michael Zagaris)

Library of Congress Cataloging-in-Publication Data

Caffrey, Scott.
The story of the Oakland Raiders / by Scott Caffrey.
p. cm. — (NFL today)
Includes index.
ISBN 978-1-58341-765-2
1. Oakland Raiders (Football team)—History—
Juvenile literature. I. Title. II. Series.

GV956.O24C35 2009
796.332'640979466—dc22   2008022696

First Edition
9 8 7 6 5 4 3 2 1

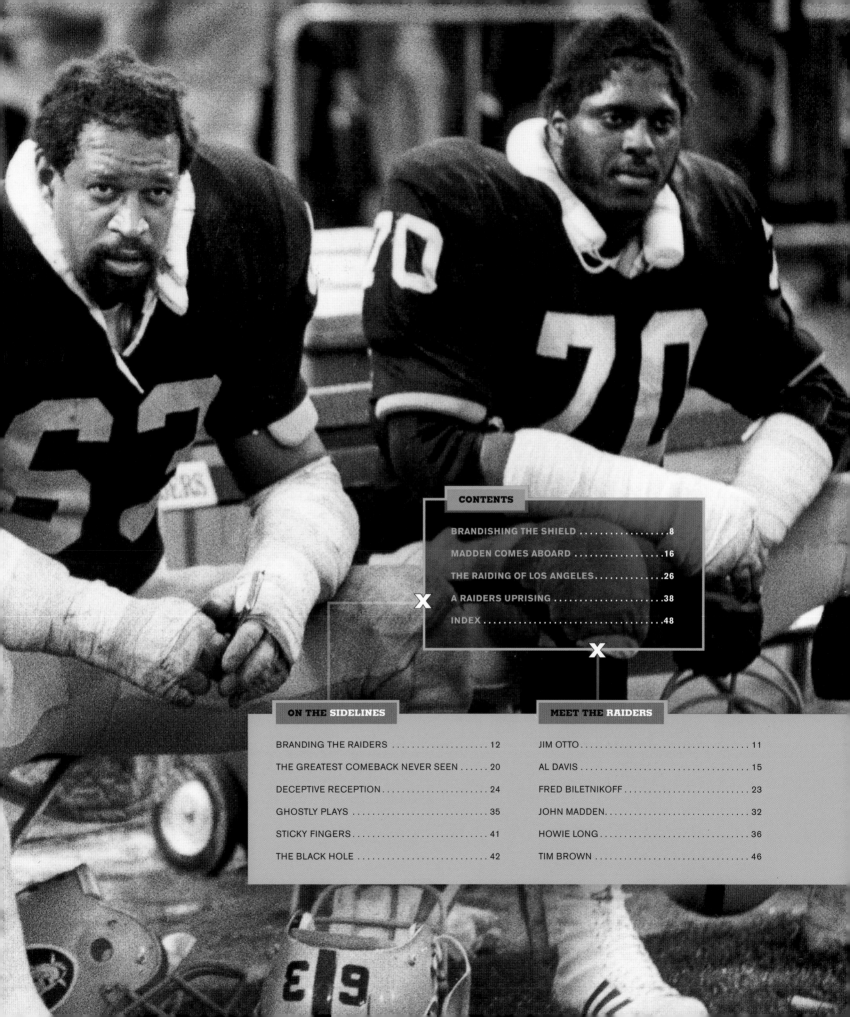

CONTENTS

ON THE SIDELINES

MEET THE RAIDERS

BRANDISHING THE SHIELD

X While lacking the glamour of neighboring San Francisco, Oakland has long boasted a robust shipping business, great weather, and—starting in 1960—a beloved pro football team.

The city of Oakland sits along the eastern side of San Francisco Bay in California. Founded in 1854 during the great California gold rush, Oakland grew slowly in the shadow of its sister city, San Francisco, but eventually became one of the busiest shipping ports in the world. Oakland is notable for being the hometown of the famous adventure writer Jack London, who is honored with a central square and a city district bearing his name. During the turbulent 1960s, Oakland became a hotbed for renegade clubs and an innovative music scene, which gave the city a kind of rebellious reputation.

By the 1950s, Oakland had only one professional sports team: the minor-league Oakland Oaks baseball team. But in 1960, the city welcomed another in the Oakland Raiders, the eighth and final team added to the fledgling American Football League (AFL). And it would not take long for the Raiders to begin developing their own reputation as rebels.

Short on funds, the Raiders got off to a rocky start. They wore second-hand uniforms and helmets without logos in an effort to save money, and their home field wasn't even in Oakland—they shared Kezar Stadium with the National Football League's (NFL) 49ers in San Francisco's Golden Gate Park. With little money to spend, team owner Chet Soda had a difficult time signing players, which forced head coach Eddie Erdelatz to scrounge for talent. Although he found some in the form of players such as quarterback Tom Flores and halfback Wayne Crow, the young Raiders went a collective 9–33 from 1960 to 1962. The future looked bleak, but Oakland had at least one star around whom it could build: center Jim Otto.

Otto was a terrific player and a steady leader whom many football fans still remember by his unusual jersey number: 00. Some NFL players and experts wondered why such a talented player would sign on with a team in the AFL, a league most people considered to be inferior to the NFL. "I could make some NFL clubs, I know," Otto said. "But it's more of an honor and distinction to be an original member of a brand-new league. "

Things improved in 1963 when Al Davis, a young coach from San Diego, took over as Oakland's head coach and general

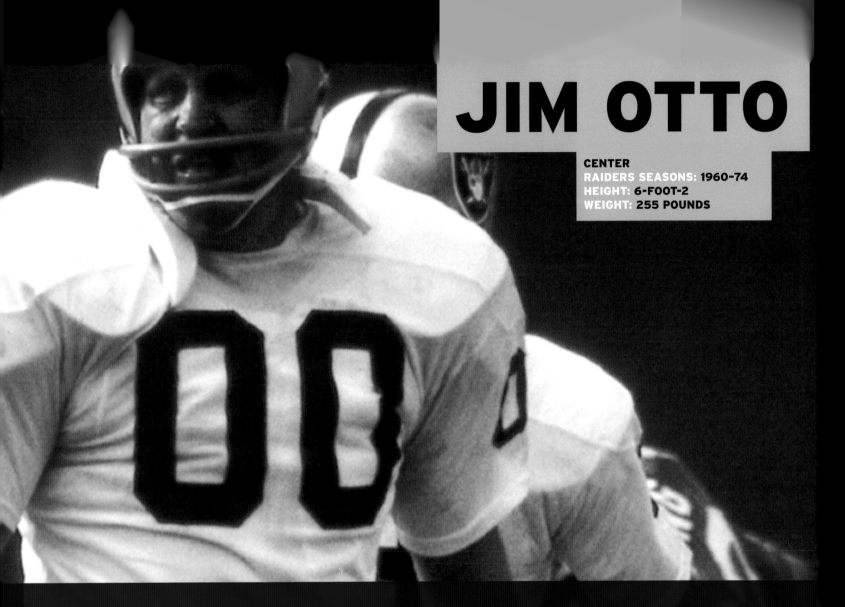

JIM OTTO

CENTER
RAIDERS SEASONS: 1960-74
HEIGHT: 6-FOOT-2
WEIGHT: 255 POUNDS

Wearing number 00 wasn't Jim Otto's only notable distinction as a player. For 10 years—the entire existence of the AFL—Otto was voted All-AFL as the best center in the league every season. "He loved to win," said Oakland quarterback George Blanda. "He led by example and he set the tempo. He gave the Raiders an image of hard discipline, hard work, and hard-nosed football." As a testament to this image, Otto played through many injuries. During a 1972 preseason game against the Buffalo Bills, he tore five ligaments in his right leg on the same play. The team doctor said Otto's season was over, and likely his career, too. But Otto not only played in the season opener three weeks later—he made the 1972 Pro Bowl. In Otto's mind, the price he paid in pain was worth it. "I was paid to play football, not hang out in the training room," he said. "That will, that drive to continue playing was derived from self-motivation." After retiring as a player, Otto remained with the team as a member of owner Al Davis's management staff.

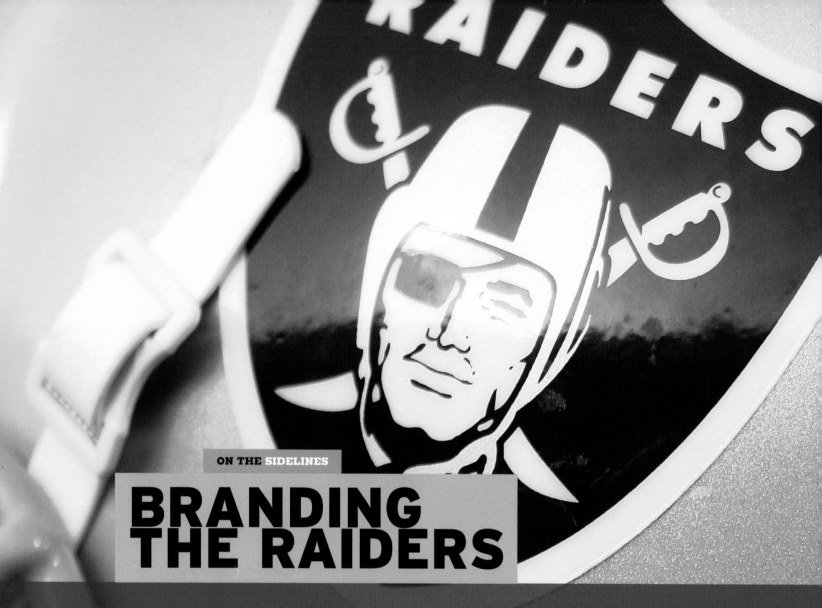

ON THE SIDELINES

BRANDING THE RAIDERS

When the Oakland Raiders franchise was founded in 1960, the team had trouble getting off the ground. With black, gold, and white hand-me-down uniforms, no helmet logo, and a 9–33 record over its first three seasons, the team had a horrible image. So when Al Davis took over, his first order of business was to forge the Raiders brand. And he started with the logo—a shield with crossed swords and a "raider," or pirate, wearing an old-time football helmet. "We all believe in the patch [logo]," Davis said. "Just like Disney says 'Mickey Mouse [is the symbol] of the entertainment world,' I believe this is the patch of the sports world. I believe the Raiders are global." Davis also trademarked his team's slogans: "Pride and Poise," "Commitment to Excellence," and "Just Win, Baby" in an all-out effort to get the Raiders into the public consciousness. But Davis knew none of it would work without on-field success, and the Raiders soon had that, becoming a powerhouse in the 1970s. "What's important is winning," he said. "In my culture, in our culture, in the Raider Culture."

manager. Davis brought big ideas and a new energy level to the young squad. One of his first goals was to build an intimidating team image that reflected the city's outsider status. He did this by outfitting his players in new uniforms of silver and black and adding a tough-looking helmet logo. "Because of Oakland's image, and the type of team image Al wanted to build, the bond was natural for us," fullback Mark van Eeghen said.

Davis instructed his team to play with two *P*s: pride and poise. "Poise is the secret," he announced. "No matter what the scoreboard says, keep your poise." With Davis running the operation, the 1963 Raiders jumped to 10–4, and he was named the AFL's Coach of the Year.

Davis also made a quick impression on the AFL's team owners. The new league was having a hard time competing with the long-established NFL, so the owners named him AFL commissioner in 1966, and he relocated to New York to try to improve the AFL's fortunes. After hiring head coach John Rauch to lead the Raiders, Davis launched a campaign against the NFL by signing many of its stars to AFL contracts. (Davis's aggressive work set in motion an NFL-AFL merger that would be completed in 1970. Because Davis himself was against the merger, the NFL would be kept to two conferences—the

National Football Conference (NFC) and the American Football

Conference (AFC)—as a compromise.)

Davis returned to Oakland late in 1966 after his brief

commissionership was completed, and he immediately shook

up the roster in search of talent that could complement

stalwart players such as wide receiver Fred Biletnikoff. He

traded for cornerback Willie Brown and young quarterback

Daryle "The Mad Bomber" Lamonica, drafted offensive guard

Gene Upshaw, and took a chance on veteran quarterback

George Blanda. By the start of the 1967 season, Oakland had

a strong team with intriguing potential.

Behind Lamonica's 34 total touchdowns, Oakland

surged to 13–1 that season. After dominating the Houston

Oilers 40–7 in the AFL Championship Game, the Raiders

marched into Super Bowl II to face legendary coach Vince

Lombardi and his NFL champion Green Bay Packers. Lamonica

and scoring-machine tight end Billy Cannon did their best, but

it wasn't enough, and the Raiders lost 33–14. Nevertheless,

the Raiders had served notice that they were now a force with

which to be reckoned.

AL DAVIS

**TEAM OWNER
RAIDERS SEASONS:
1963-PRESENT**

Al Davis never played a single down of professional football. But after taking over the Oakland Raiders in 1963, he became the living embodiment of the franchise. To him, image and style were just as important as winning, and his devotion to the "Silver and Black" was all-consuming. This was reflected even in his wardrobe, which was made up almost entirely of black, white, and silver warm-up suits (and not just because he was colorblind). Davis almost always wore a Super Bowl ring on each hand, dark sunglasses, and a slicked-back hairstyle—a look that reinforced the maverick image that he always preferred. So when he once said, "I'm not really a part of society," there was some truth to it. "His life is the Raiders," explained former special teams coach Steve Ortmayer. "That's not a statement to be taken lightly, like a lot of people's life is what they do. It's to an extent he has never taken a day off from the Raiders. Never." **Davis** was the only person in the NFL ever to have served in six different positions—player personnel assistant, assistant coach, head coach, general manager, league commissioner, and the principal owner of a team.

MADDEN COMES ABOARD

X--------

After Oakland lost to the New York Jets in the 1968 AFL Championship Game, Coach Rauch took the Buffalo Bills' head coaching job. So, in 1969, Davis handed the head-coaching reins over to linebackers coach John Madden, who immediately instilled a different attitude in the locker room. "I had a philosophy," Madden explained. "I really liked my players. I liked them as people. I made a point to talk to each player personally every day.... You can be intense and competitive and all that, but try to remember to laugh and have fun. It's just a football game."

X John Madden's belief in listening to the input of such players as quarterback Daryle Lamonica helped make him a popular coach—and took the Raiders to a new level of success.

The Raiders went 12–1–1 under their rookie head coach and drubbed the Oilers 56–7 in the playoffs before being ousted 17–7 by the rival Kansas City Chiefs in the next round. With a Lamonica and Blanda quarterback tandem, Oakland won the new AFC West Division title in 1970 and reached the AFC Championship Game against the Baltimore Colts. The game started close, but after Blanda threw two late end-zone interceptions, and legendary Colts quarterback Johnny Unitas launched a 68-yard scoring pass, the Colts prevailed 27–17.

After a second straight 8–4–2 record in 1971, the Raiders improved to 10–3–1 in 1972. In a playoff game that year against the Pittsburgh Steelers, the Raiders had all but won when a routine collision turned into an improbable loss.

X Safety Jack Tatum (number 31) and the rest of the Raiders defense were holding down the Steelers in the 1972 playoffs before Franco Harris's incredible touchdown reception.

Backup quarterback Ken Stabler replaced an ill Lamonica at the start of the fourth quarter and showed fans why he was nicknamed "The Snake" when he scrambled for a 30-yard score to stake Oakland to a 7–6 lead. Then, on fourth-down-and-10 with 22 seconds left, Steelers quarterback Terry Bradshaw threw a desperation pass to running back John "Frenchy" Fuqua. Raiders safety Jack Tatum collided with Fuqua, and the ball ricocheted backward. Pittsburgh running back Franco Harris caught the deflection and rumbled 42

X Quarterback Ken Stabler became known for his cool leadership and precise passing on the field—and a wild, partying lifestyle off of it.

ON THE SIDELINES

THE GREATEST COMEBACK NEVER SEEN

On November 17, 1968, Oakland played the New York Jets in a matchup that featured two of the AFL's marquee teams and 10 future Hall-of-Famers. But that's not why it was voted the 10th Most Memorable Game of the Century by fans on the NFL.com Web site. Rather, it's because Oakland's stunning comeback win was seen by few fans. Following the 4:00 P.M. game, the NBC television network was set to air the movie *Heidi*, based on the popular children's book, at 7:00 P.M. So when New York took a 32–29 lead with just over a minute remaining, NBC figured the game was effectively over and switched to *Heidi* everywhere except on the West Coast. Viewers who had hoped to see the end of the game were disappointed—but not as disappointed as when they found out the Raiders scored two late touchdowns to win 43–32. NBC was so bombarded by complaints that the network was forced to issue a public apology. "Probably the most significant factor to come out of *Heidi* was, whatever you do, you better not leave an NFL football game," said Val Pinchbeck, the NFL's former chief of broadcasting.

yards for the winning score on the so-called "Immaculate Reception," and Oakland was left stunned by the 13–7 loss.

The next year, Coach Madden named Stabler his starter—a position the gritty southpaw would hold for the rest of the 1970s. During those years, Oakland also became known for its fearsome defense. Tatum was nicknamed "The Assassin" for his frighteningly fierce tackles; Ted Hendricks was a versatile, 6-foot-7 linebacker nicknamed the "Mad Stork"; and cornerback Willie Brown didn't need a nickname to become the club's all-time interceptions leader (39).

With this impressive lineup, the Silver and Black reached the AFC Championship Game in 1973, 1974, and 1975—and lost every time. To make matters even worse, each opponent went on to win the Super Bowl. By 1976, the Raiders had a reputation as a team that couldn't win the big one.

But Davis refused to give up on Madden, and Madden refused to give up on his players. With Stabler tossing 27 touchdown passes and the defense stronger than ever, Oakland went 13–1 in 1976. Its only stumble was a lopsided 48–17 loss to the New England Patriots. In the playoffs, the Raiders exacted revenge on the Patriots with a dramatic, 24–21 victory that entailed two fourth-quarter Oakland touchdowns. After demolishing Pittsburgh 24–7 in the AFC

Championship Game, the Raiders faced the Minnesota Vikings in Super Bowl XI.

Tackle Art Shell and guard Gene Upshaw made the left side of the Raiders' offensive line dominant. This road-grading tandem manhandled Pro Bowl defensive linemen Alan Page and Jim Marshall, part of Minnesota's vaunted "Purple People Eaters" line. They blew open holes for van Eeghen and halfback Clarence Davis as the Raiders ran for 266 yards on a whopping 52 carries for a 32–14 victory and their first world championship. Biletnikoff was named the game's Most Valuable Player (MVP), but the conquest was truly a team effort.

The Raiders came back strong in 1977 with an 11–3 record, but they were shaky in the playoffs. In the first round against the Baltimore Colts, Raiders kicker Errol Mann sent the contest into overtime with a game-tying field goal. After a scoreless first overtime, Stabler finally hit tight end Dave Casper for the winning score in the second overtime. Although the AFC Championship Game versus the Denver Broncos was a tight affair, Stabler threw an interception that contributed to a 20–17 Oakland loss.

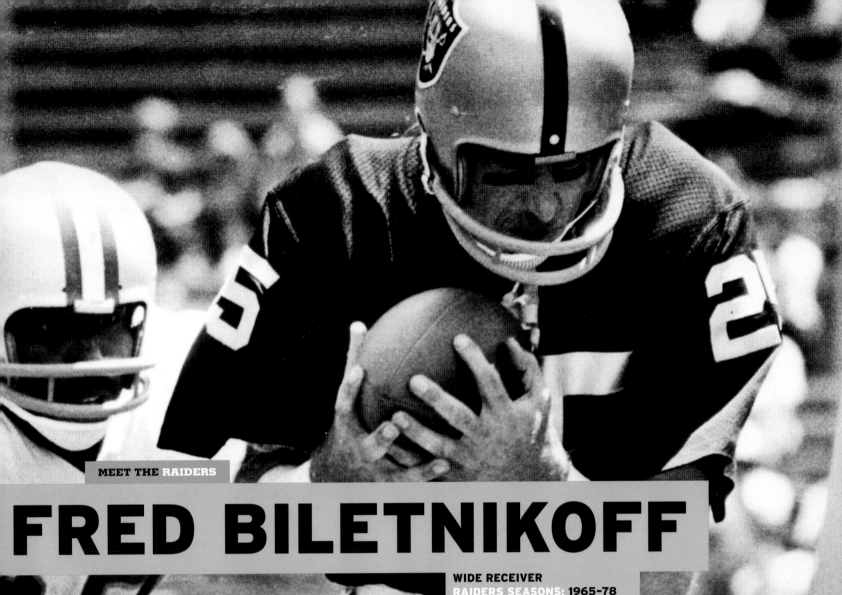

FRED BILETNIKOFF

WIDE RECEIVER
RAIDERS SEASONS: 1965-78
HEIGHT: 6-FOOT-1
WEIGHT: 190 POUNDS

Al Davis always preferred a vertical passing offense—in other words, quarterbacks with powerful arms and speedy receivers that could catch long bombs downfield. But he made an exception for slow-footed Fred Biletnikoff. "We felt, with our approach to total pass offense, that speed wasn't the only consideration," Davis said. In Biletnikoff, the Raiders got a tough, hard-nosed, go-to receiver who was unafraid to run over the middle of the field where linebackers might crush him. A precise route-runner with superb hand-eye coordination, Biletnikoff was known as a player who could catch even the worst passes. "The guy can catch anything he can touch," Raiders coach John Madden said. "That's no accident. Some receivers might catch 15 passes in practice. Fred will stick around and catch 100." Biletnikoff excelled every Sunday, but he seemed to find an extra gear in the playoffs. In 19 postseason games, he set NFL records with 70 catches, 1,167 yards, and 10 touchdowns. Biletnikoff caught 40 or more passes in 10 consecutive seasons, an NFL record he shares with Hall of Fame receiver Raymond Berry of the Baltimore Colts.

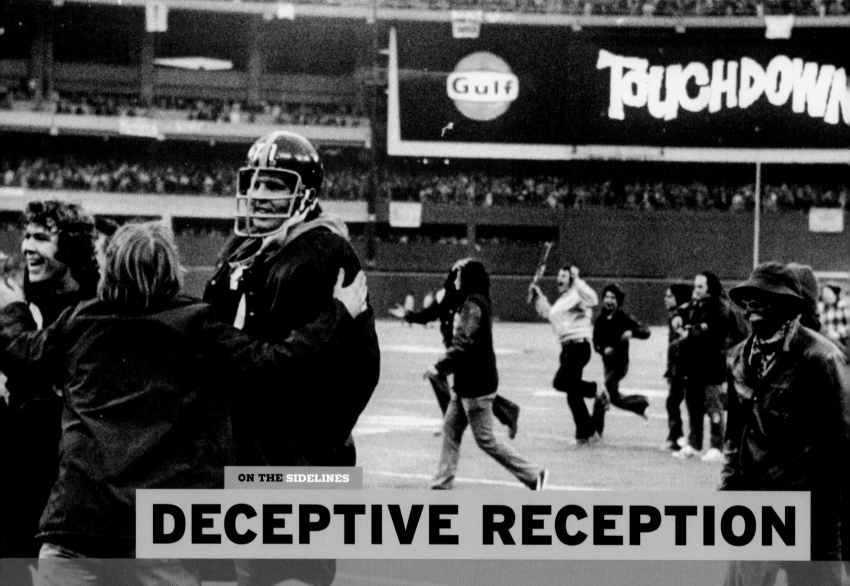

DECEPTIVE RECEPTION

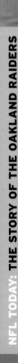

If there's one play throughout history that angers the Oakland Raiders the most, it's the one that most people know as the "Immaculate Reception." In the final seconds of a 1972 playoff game, Raiders safety Jack Tatum went to break up a pass to the Steelers' Frenchy Fuqua, drilling Fuqua and popping the ball in the air. When Fuqua's trailing teammate, Franco Harris, caught it and scored a touchdown, Raiders defenders assumed that Fuqua had hit the ball to Harris—an illegal play at the time—so the play should have been ruled incomplete. However, no official had a clear view of the play, so referee Fred Swearingen spoke with Art McNally, the NFL's supervisor of officials. At the time, instant replay was not used by NFL officials. However, it is believed that McNally viewed the play on a television screen in the press box, after which Swearingen called it a touchdown. "It remains the most incredible, implausible finish to a football game that didn't involve a marching band running onto the field," Oakland center Jim Otto said. "It also was the birth of television instant replay." To this day, many Raiders players on that 1972 team maintain that Pittsburgh won on an illegal play.

The Raiders went 9–7 in each of the next two seasons and missed the playoffs, and then Madden retired in 1979 to pursue a broadcasting career. But what a decade it had been—Oakland won the AFC West six times, made the playoffs seven times, and earned a lasting reputation as a team willing to sign troublemakers, outcasts, and aging stars and mold them into winners.

X Cornerback Lester Hayes just missed Oakland's 1976 championship, arriving as a rookie in 1977 and becoming an annual Pro-Bowler in the early '80s.

THE RAIDING OF LOS ANGELES

Under new coach Tom Flores, a former Raiders quarterback, Oakland went 11–5 in 1980. The two players most responsible for this success were cornerback Lester Hayes and quarterback Jim Plunkett. Hayes picked off an incredible 13 interceptions during the season and 5 more in the playoffs. Plunkett was a veteran backup whose NFL career had seemed finished when he joined Oakland in 1978. After Oakland lost three of its first five games in 1980, and starting quarterback Dan Pastorini went down with a broken leg, Flores called on Plunkett, who guided the Raiders to 9 wins in their next 11 games. After winning three playoff games, Oakland become the first Wild Card team ever to reach the Super Bowl.

Few experts gave the Raiders a chance against the powerful Philadelphia Eagles, but Oakland had already beaten the odds. Completing both the Raiders' incredible comeback and his own, Plunkett tossed a Super Bowl-record 80-yard touchdown pass to fullback Kenny King on Oakland's second possession. Plunkett's 261 passing yards and 3 touchdown

Quarterback Jim Plunkett won the 1970 Heisman Trophy as college football's best player but struggled to find stardom in the pro ranks until arriving in Oakland at age 32. **X**

passes propelled Oakland to a 27–10 win and earned him MVP honors.

In 1981, the Raiders uncharacteristically lost three straight shutouts early on and limped to a 7–9 record. Then, before a 1982 season that was shortened by a players' strike, Davis relocated the Raiders to Los Angeles to better capitalize on the franchise's nationwide popularity in the larger Southern California market.

The Raiders' transition to L.A. was made easier with the drafting of Marcus Allen, a fast and shifty running back who had just won the Heisman Trophy as college football's best player at the local University of Southern California. Allen rushed for 697 yards, caught passes for 401 more, and scored 14 total touchdowns to win the NFL Rookie of the Year award.

The Raiders' defense also got a makeover when defensive end Howie Long forced his way into the starting lineup and the team signed Cleveland Browns defensive tackle Lyle "Darth Raider" Alzado. Along with fleet-footed linebacker Rod Martin, the rugged "D" quickly won new L.A. fans over.

In 1983, the Raiders went 12–4 and returned to the Super Bowl, which Allen turned into his own personal showcase with 191 rushing yards and 2 touchdowns—including a sensational 74-yard scoring run. "I was picking myself up off the ground," Raiders guard Mickey Marvin remembered, "then I looked around and a rocket went through!" Allen and the Raiders trounced the Washington Redskins 38–9 for their third world title. Although Allen would remain a Raiders star for many seasons, few performances would match Super Bowl XVIII's. "This has to be the greatest feeling of my life," he said. "I've been to the Rose Bowl. I've won the Heisman Trophy. But nothing is sweeter than this."

The Raiders compiled winning records over the next two seasons but were bounced in the first round of the playoffs

X Marcus Allen earned a reputation as one of the most versatile halfbacks in history, a swift, slippery runner whether taking handoffs or catching passes.

MEET THE RAIDERS

JOHN MADDEN

COACH
RAIDERS SEASONS: 1969-78

As a junior offensive lineman at California Polytechnic State University in 1958, John Madden was drafted by the Philadelphia Eagles. But his playing career ended before it started when he injured his knee in training camp his rookie year. The injury turned out to be a blessing in disguise. Madden would arrive early before practice to get treatment, only to find Eagles quarterback Norm Van Brocklin watching game films. Eventually, Van Brocklin asked Madden to assist him with play breakdowns. "I learned more about football than ever before," Madden said. "Van Brocklin was a bright guy, and he taught me all about the passing game and how to attack a defense." Once he learned his injury was career-ending, the genial, talkative Madden decided to become a coach. He took over as head coach of the Raiders in 1969 and held the position for a decade. Under his stewardship, Oakland never suffered a losing season. Following his coaching tenure, Madden became a successful broadcaster and earned fame for his custom-made Madden Cruiser bus, his annual "All-Madden" teams," and his popular *Madden NFL* video game franchise.

each time. Even though Los Angeles featured a number of exceptional players—including tight end Todd Christensen and cornerback Mike Haynes—by 1987, things were getting ugly. Flores and preeminent punter Ray Guy both retired. Then the team's new coach, Mike Shanahan, clashed with Davis's overbearing personality and would last less than two seasons.

But the excitement level rose with the arrival of another Heisman Trophy winner: running back Vincent "Bo" Jackson. Originally drafted by the Tampa Bay Buccaneers in 1986,

X Ray Guy is regarded by some as the greatest punter of all time; not a single one of his 1,049 career punts was returned for a touchdown.

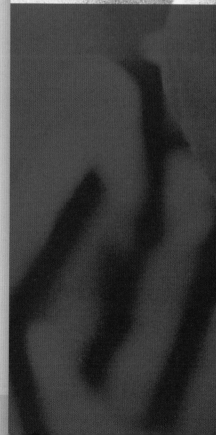

X Bo Jackson's career was brief but brilliant; his knack for violently flattening defenders made him one of the biggest attractions in football.

Jackson decided to instead fulfill his lifelong dream of playing professional baseball and signed with the Kansas City Royals. Then, in 1987, he decided he would play both sports and signed with the Raiders.

Few experts thought Jackson could successfully play two professional sports, but he proved the critics wrong during a memorable Monday Night Football game against the Seattle Seahawks on his 25th birthday. Jackson ran for 221 yards and scored 3 touchdowns, including a breathtaking 91-yard

GHOSTLY PLAYS

Oakland tight end Dave "The Ghost" Casper was responsible for not one, but three historic plays. The first two came in a 1977 AFC playoff game against the Baltimore Colts. Casper's "Ghost to the Post" play, in which he ran downfield toward the goalpost, resulted in a 42-yard reception that set up a game-tying field goal to force overtime. Then, in the second overtime, he caught a 10-yard, game-winning touchdown. Early the next season, he helped complete a play that became known as "The Holy Roller." Oakland was trailing the San Diego Chargers 20–14 on the last play of the game when quarterback Ken Stabler intentionally fumbled, and Raiders running back Pete Banaszak batted the ball toward the goal line. Casper then awkwardly fell on it in the end zone to score the game-winning touchdown. "It would've been nicer to do it a little smoother," Casper joked, "with a little more skill and like a dancer or something." The famous play brought about an NFL rule change; beginning the next season, only the initial fumbler could legally advance the ball on fourth down or inside the final two minutes of a half.

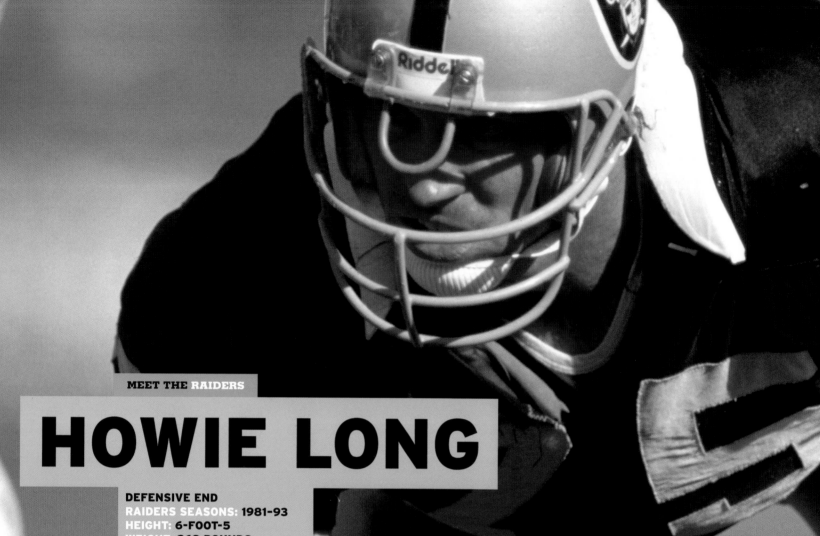

HOWIE LONG

DEFENSIVE END
RAIDERS SEASONS: 1981–93
HEIGHT: 6-FOOT-5
WEIGHT: 268 POUNDS

If it wasn't for Oakland defensive line coach Earl Leggett, Howie Long might not have worn a Raiders jersey or built a Hall of Fame career that included eight Pro Bowls. "Nobody was really after him [in the 1981 NFL Draft]," Leggett said. "But I didn't want to take a chance. I was pushing him real hard on draft day." After the Raiders drafted him, Long became Leggett's personal project in training camp. "Every day at practice, it was a new position," Long said. "I couldn't understand what he was doing at the time." What Leggett was doing was taking advantage of Long's strength, quickness, and intense desire to excel. And he helped turn Long into one of the most versatile linemen in the league. Although he consistently ranked near the top of the NFL in sack totals, Long played the run just as well. "There are guys who are bigger, guys who are stronger, guys who are meaner," said teammate Matt Millen, a linebacker. "But none of them puts it together the way he does. Nobody has his blend. He does everything." After retiring, Long became a highly regarded NFL television analyst.

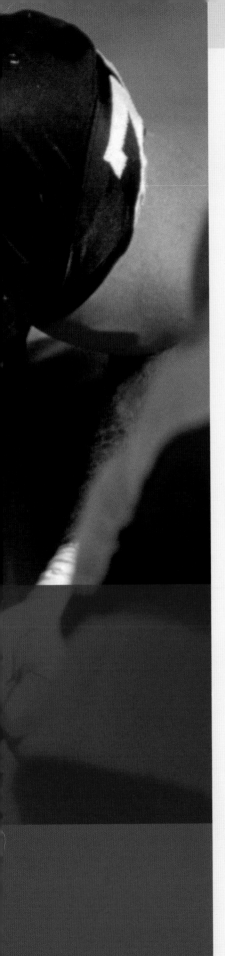

scoring sprint and a bulldozing romp over much-hyped rookie linebacker Brian Bosworth.

    Still, the Raiders needed more talent. And they found some in the form of Tim Brown from the University of Notre Dame. The first wide receiver ever to win the Heisman Trophy, Brown's prowess as a kick returner made him a dangerous weapon. Plus, he arrived in Los Angeles with a helpful advantage: Steve Beuerlein, his quarterback at Notre Dame, was also on the Raiders roster. Although Jackson and Brown racked up some impressive statistics, wins were still in short supply in Los Angeles.

X From his first Raiders season (1988) to his last (2003), Tim Brown was a star, a threat to score any time he caught a pass or returned a kick.

A RAIDERS UPRISING

NFL TODAY: THE STORY OF THE OAKLAND RAIDERS

X Cornerback
Charles Woodson
wasted no time in
joining the ranks of
outstanding Raiders
defensive backs, going
to the Pro Bowl in each
of his first four NFL
seasons (1998–2001).

Looking to stabilize the team, Davis hired former star Art Shell as head coach in 1989. Shell patiently coached according to Raiders tradition, emphasizing a strong passing offense and a stout defense. He relied on leaders such as standout guard Steve Wisniewski to help solidify the offense, while defensive end Greg Townsend and cornerback Terry McDaniel galvanized the defense. These players led the Raiders to some solid seasons in the early '90s, including postseason appearances in 1990 and 1991.

Unfortunately for Raiders fans, Jackson's bright career ended when he injured his hip in a 20–10 playoff win over the Cincinnati Bengals after the 1990 season. Further tests revealed a degenerative bone disease. After only four seasons, one of the most electrifying players the league had ever witnessed was forced into retirement.

After some ups and downs in Los Angeles, Davis decided to move his franchise back to Oakland in 1995. "Raider Nation," a name given to Oakland's many passionate football fans, enthusiastically welcomed their team home. Despite the Raiders' middling 8–8 record that season under new head coach Mike White, "The Black Hole" (the Oakland Coliseum's seating section for the most enthusiastic fans) was a raucous place once again.

In 1998, after back-to-back losing seasons, the Raiders needed a new identity, so Davis hired 34-year-old Jon Gruden as head coach. Although Gruden was younger than some of his players, he had a fiery personality, and his Raiders made the next few seasons memorable ones. Veteran quarterback Rich Gannon led an increasingly powerful offense, while young cornerback Charles Woodson emerged as a defensive standout. After back-to-back 8–8 seasons in 1998 and 1999, the Raiders jumped to 12–4 in 2000. After shutting out the Miami Dolphins 27–0 in the playoffs, they lost to the Baltimore Ravens 16–3 in the AFC Championship Game.

The next year, Oakland went 10–6 before losing to the New England Patriots in a snowy playoff game that earned lasting infamy. The Raiders appeared to seal a 13–10 victory late in the fourth quarter when Woodson sacked Patriots quarterback Tom Brady and forced a fumble that the defense recovered. However, after reviewing instant replay, referee Walt Coleman overturned the play on "The Tuck Rule" (stating that Brady's arm was moving forward and that the fumble was, therefore, technically an incomplete pass). Patriots kicker Adam Vinatieri promptly kicked a 45-yard field goal to send the game into overtime, and then won it with another clutch field goal.

STICKY FINGERS

Over the years, the Raiders have earned a reputation as a team willing to try just about anything to gain a winning edge. So when equipment manager Dick Romanski introduced "Stickum," a gluelike spray, in the mid-1970s, receiver Fred Biletnikoff applied it to any part of his body and uniform that could help him catch balls—hands, arms, jersey, and pants. But not until Biletnikoff introduced it to rookie cornerback Lester Hayes in 1977 did Stickum take on a life of its own. Hayes started out as a converted linebacker just trying to make the team. And while he wasn't the only other player to use Stickum, by 1980 he was arguably the most successful. That year, Hayes intercepted 18 total passes and became the NFL Defensive Player of the Year. "The sole focus of our team was to win consistently," said Hayes. "Our attitude was that if we could get away with something, we were going to do it." The Raiders didn't get away with it for long. Stickum was banned after the 1980 season, and Hayes was cited as the main reason.

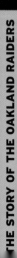
THE BLACK HOLE

Affectionately referred to as "Raider Nation," fans of the Oakland Raiders are some of the most unusual and passionate in all of professional sports. "We are Raider fans," wrote fan/author Craig Parker. "We pretend to know who these guys [players] are. They're the Silver-and-Black Gang. And they will gang tackle as soon as look at you. And we know what they're after. They want an AFC West Division title with home-field advantage throughout the playoffs." The most fanatical members of Raider Nation are known for occupying "The Black Hole," which encompasses seating sections 104, 105, 106, and 107 of the Oakland Coliseum. The spot is frequented by arguably the rowdiest and most colorful fans in the league. Some dress up in ornate costumes that make them look like futuristic football warriors, complete with black and silver makeup, war helmets, and spiked shoulder pads. "It's amazing," Raiders tight end Rickey Dudley said. "You know why they call it the Raider Nation? Because it's nationwide. Miami, New York, wherever. You're part of the Raider Nation. It's so large. They say Dallas is America's Team. Well, I'm not so sure about that. The Raiders are beloved."

After the 2001 season, disagreements between Davis and Gruden reached a head. Davis then made the unusual decision to trade Gruden to the Tampa Bay Buccaneers, who sent cash and four draft picks to Oakland in return. Although many Raiders fans lamented the loss of the popular Gruden, the 2002 Raiders came back stronger than ever under new coach Bill Callahan. Gannon had the finest season of his career, passing for an incredible 4,689 yards and 26 touchdowns to win the NFL MVP award.

The Raiders then won two playoff games to reach the Super Bowl for the first time in 19 years, where they faced former coach Gruden and his Buccaneers. "There is going to be a natural rivalry in this Super Bowl, and that's not all bad," Raiders defensive end Trace Armstrong said. "I thought he [Gruden] was an excellent coach.... But that doesn't mean we don't want to beat him." Unfortunately for Oakland, Gruden's inside knowledge of the Raiders seemed to give Tampa Bay an edge. The Bucs became the first team to score three defensive touchdowns in a Super Bowl as they demolished Oakland 48–21.

That defeat seemed to send the Raiders into a tailspin, as they would not achieve a winning record over the next six seasons. Despite the best efforts of kicker Sebastian

TIM BROWN

WIDE RECEIVER
RAIDERS SEASONS: 1988–2003
HEIGHT: 6 FEET
WEIGHT: 195 POUNDS

Throughout his entire 16-year career with the Raiders, "Touchdown Timmy" Brown remained a consistent star. The first wide receiver ever to win the prestigious Heisman Trophy, Brown made an immediate impact in his rookie season. He led the NFL in kickoff returns, and combining those yards with his punt return, receiving, and even rushing gains, Brown amassed a total of 2,317 yards, which remains an NFL rookie record. The self-proclaimed "Mr. Raider" holds most of the team's receiving records, and his 240 games played and 9 Pro Bowl appearances wearing the Silver and Black are the most in franchise history. Brown never ceased to amaze teammates and coaches with his great instincts and ability to learn new offensive plays. "We call him 'The Natural,'" coach Jon Gruden said. "You tell him one time, you show him one time, and you can expect perfection." Ever the perfectionist, Brown decided to leave the team in 2003 rather than accept a reduced role on the offense. "When you've played at the level I've played at," Brown explained, "it's tough to sit on the sidelines waving a towel."

Janikowski, and despite having star receiver Randy Moss on the roster for two of those years, their best season in that span was a 5–11 finish in 2004.

In 2007, Davis shook up the franchise and made headlines when he hired 31-year-old Lane Kiffin as the youngest head coach in the history of the NFL. Then, after the team went 4–12 in 2007 and started 1–3 in 2008, the owner made headlines again by firing Kiffin. Although the losses kept piling up as the Raiders lingered near the AFC West cellar, fans clung to the hope that such young players as tough linebacker Kirk Morrison, huge quarterback JaMarcus Russell, and speedy running back Darren McFadden would soon carry Oakland back to its rightful place among the NFL elite.

The history of the Oakland Raiders is one of the NFL's great stories. They have assembled the best winning percentage in pro football since the 1963 season and won three Super Bowls. Author Mark Ribowsky once wrote that the Raiders were a group of "odds and ends, oddities and irregulars, factory seconds and seeming chain-gang escapees." It's an image the team's players are proud of and will continue to wear as a badge of honor as they chase their next world championship.

INDEX